Can you guess the dangling participle for this image?

For the answer and the corrected sentence go to VanitaBooks.com

Profits

*All net profits from this book will be donated to
charitable organizations, with a gentle preference towards
people with my husband's disease – multiple sclerosis.*

Vanita Oelschlager

Acknowledgments

Mike DeSantis

Jennie Levy Smith

Kristin Blackwood

Sheila Tarr

Lynda Durrant

Carol Riddle

Kurt Landefeld

Carol Landefeld

Text by Vanita Oelschlager.
Illustrations by Mike DeSantis.
Design by Jennie Levy Smith,
Trio Design & Marketing Communications Inc.
Printed in the U.S.A.
ISBN 978-1-938164-02-6 Hardcover
ISBN 978-1-938164-03-3 Paperback

www.VanitaBooks.com

Don't DANGLE YOUR PARTICIPLE

by Vanita Oelschlager
art mike Desantis

This book is dedicated to my sweet
granddaughter, Daphne...always smiling.
Vanita Oelschlager

This book is dedicated to aspiring writers.
Mike DeSantis

DON'T DANGLE YOUR PARTICIPLE

What on earth is a *participle* and how does it *dangle*?

Okay. Okay. Let's start at the beginning.

A *participle* is a **verb** that acts like an **adjective**.

Let's use the verb **growl**. The *participle* is the verb ending with an **ing** and sometimes an **ed**. Growling is the *participle*.

growl — *I'm the verb. I perform an action.*

growling — *I'm the participle. I end in ing or sometimes ed.*

How does the *participle* act like an *adjective*?

Well I am glad you asked. The *participle* comes before a *noun* to modify it. That is a fancy way of having the *participle* better clarify what the *noun* means.

Wait a minute. You are losing me.

The *participle* **growling** might come before the word **lion** to describe to your reader what kind of lion we are talking about. Are we talking about a **sleeping** lion? Or a **yawning** lion? No, we are talking about a **growling** lion.

sleeping lion

yawning lion

growling lion

Still with me?

So now we know what a *verb* and a *participle* are, but sentences are made of more than just *verbs* and *participles*. They have, *nouns*, *pronouns*, *adverbs*, *adjectives*, *prepositions*, *conjunctions*, and *interjections* to name a few.

When you add in all these other parts of a sentence it is easy for your *participle*, **growling,** to get lost from the *noun*, **lion,** and end up in the wrong part of your sentence.

Here is an example of a participle that has lost its way.

Growling as they ate, the children gathered around the lions' cage.

Oops. The *participle* has lost its way and now it is modifying the wrong noun. It is modifying the **children** instead of the **lions**.

Here we will help our *participle* get back to the right place in the sentence and to modify **lions** instead of the **children**.

Here you go.

Growling as they ate, the lions attracted the children to their cage.

Now **growling** is modifying **lions** and the *participle* has found its way. Yippee!

Growling as they ate, the children gathered around the lions' cage.

Growling as they ate, the lions attracted the children to their cage.

While *riding* his skateboard in the park,
a deer almost ran into Lester.

While *riding* his skateboard in the park,
Lester was almost hit by a deer.

Running with the Thanksgiving turkey in his mouth, Marvin chased the dog around the kitchen.

Running with the Thanksgiving turkey in his mouth, the dog was chased around the kitchen by Marvin.

Carried away on a gust of wind, Susie frantically grabbed for the balloons.

Carried away on a gust of wind, the balloons were grabbed frantically by Susie.

Eating like a pig, my cake
was gone in seconds.

Eating like a pig, I finished my cake in seconds.

Driving to the top of the
mountain, a large turtle
was nearly squashed.

Driving to the top of the mountain, our car nearly squashed a large turtle.

Wrestling a giant, hairy fly, Simon was fascinated by the spider.

Wrestling a giant, hairy fly,
the spider fascinated Simon.

Melting in the hot sun, Ida rushed to finish her ice cream.

Melting in the hot sun, the ice cream had to be finished quickly by Ida.

The Author and Illustrator

Vanita Oelschlager is a wife, mother, grandmother, philanthropist, former teacher, current caregiver, author and poet. She is a graduate of the University of Mount Union in Alliance, Ohio, where she currently serves as a Trustee. Vanita is also Writer in Residence for the Literacy Program at The University of Akron. She and her husband Jim received a *Lifetime Achievement Award* from the National Multiple Sclerosis Society in 2006. She won the Congressional *Angels in Adoption™ Award* for the State of Ohio in 2007 and was named *National Volunteer of the Year* by the MS society in 2008. She was honored as 2009 *Woman Philanthropist of the Year* by the United Way of Summit County. In May 2011, Vanita received an honorary Doctor of Humane Letters from the University of Mount Union. In 2013, Vanita joined *The LeBron James Family Foundation* to serve on its Advisory Board.

Mike DeSantis creates puzzles and illustrations for children's books and magazines. He attended the Cleveland Institute of Art and received a BS in Management from Case Western Reserve University. Mike lives near Cleveland with his wife, three wonderful children, and two barking dogs.

About the Art

STEP 1

The idea is sketched out in pencil on to paper.

STEP 2

The picture is traced onto heavy watercolor paper. Brown and black ink mixed with water are used to paint in the outlines and shadows.

STEP 3

The colors are added with watercolor paints.

STEP 4

The picture is finished with a few more touches of color, and some dark brown ink for the lines.